Rebecca Manley P
with Dick Molenhouse

EMPOWERED

Equipping everyone for relational evangelism

- HANDBOOK -

Empowered

www.beckypippertministries.org

Published by:
The Good Book Company Ltd
Blenheim House, 1 Blenheim Road, Epsom, Surrey, KT19 9AP, UK
Tel: +44 (0) 208 942 0880
Email: info@thegoodbook.com

Published in association with the literary agency of
Wolgemuth & Associates, Inc.

Websites:
North America: www.thegoodbook.com
UK and Europe: www.thegoodbook.co.uk
Australia: www.thegoodbook.com.au
New Zealand: www.thegoodbook.co.nz

thegoodbook COMPANY

Becky Pippert MINISTRIES

ISBN: 9781784981051

Design by André Parker

Printed in Turkey

CONTENTS

Welcome 5

1. Inadequacy is Compulsory 7
2. The Cross: The Mess and the Miracle 15
3. Facing Our Fears 23
4. It's all about Relationships 31
5. Cultivating Curiosity 39
6. The Gospel: Content and Response 47
7. Introducing the Irresistible Jesus 55

EXTRA RESOURCES

Praying Powerfully 69

Big Questions 71

Helpful Ways to Outline the Gospel 73

Apologetics: Resources for Answering Tough Questions 77

WELCOME TO EMPOWERED

I was recently interviewed on an American Christian radio show where people could call in. The subject was evangelism, and ten minutes into the interview the entire phone board lit up with callers from across the country. The comments were revealing.

Every caller spoke of someone they deeply cared about who was not a Christian.

While they longed for their friend to come to Christ, they felt completely inadequate in how to reach them.

Their fears were very similar: How do I raise the topic of faith naturally? What if I offend them or they reject me? What if they raise questions I can't answer?

Everyone essentially asked the same thing: How do I reach people in today's increasingly secular culture? As one caller put it:

"Jesus didn't suggest we share the good news—he commanded us to. But how do we communicate the eternal Christ in our secular, ever-changing world?"

Never has there been a greater need to share Christ with the world (starting with our own neighbors)—yet never have believers seemed more ill equipped.

And that is why I am so excited to welcome you to *Empowered*—a course that equips ordinary Christians for personal evangelism. For the past thirteen years Dick and I have conducted evangelism-training conferences and been part of evangelistic initiatives around the world. For the first six years we ministered on every continent (apart from Antarctica!). Then for the next seven, we were focused primarily on Europe. Europe has long been considered the most challenging place for the gospel in the world—yet we have seen amazing fruit as Christians have reached out in even the most unlikely places.

Empowered is the fruit of all these years of working right around the world, of motivating and equipping ordinary Christians to share their faith with those around them.

It is imperative that we know how to effectively communicate the gospel. We need to get beyond one-size-fits-all techniques. We need to learn to communicate the truth in a way that is also loving. Yet we need to remember, even as we seek to show Christ's compassionate love, still to share Christ's gospel truth.

We need to recover the "Jesus way"—the biblical way—by creatively and persuasively sharing God's truth in the context of authentic relationships and community, so that people may become radical, missional disciples.

So *Empowered* is for you—especially if you feel inept or inadequate about being a witness for Christ. We wrote this course for you—for you to become empowered to talk about Jesus in everyday conversations in your ordinary life. Thank you for making the time to join us—we'll be praying that the truths you hear, the Bible passages you study, the discussions you have, the thinking you do and the prayers you share will change you, and so change the lives and eternities of those around you.

Thanks,

Becky Dick

1 INADEQUACY IS COMPULSORY

REFLECTION: AS YOU BEGIN...

What three words best describe how you feel about evangelism?

What do you hope to get out of doing this course?

BIBLE STUDY

Read 1 Corinthians 2 v 1-5

1. How did Paul feel about sharing the gospel with people in Corinth?

2. What did he focus on talking about? Why, do you think?

3. What did Paul's message not come with, and what did accompany it (v 4-5)?

Why was that a good thing for the faith of the people who did listen to him?

4. When we feel weak about talking to others about Jesus, how is Paul both an encouragement and a challenge to us?

1. Our Motivation for Witness—God the Father

Jesus was criticized for mingling with sinners, and responded by telling three stories (Luke 15):

- ~ The Lost Sheep
- ~ The Lost Coin
- ~ Two Lost Sons

God searches for the lost and rejoices when they are found. He loves people, and so must we.

2. Our Model for Witness—Jesus

The eternal Son of God came to live on earth as a weak human being!

God's glory and power is revealed through human weakness (1 Corinthians 2 v 3-5).

Jesus' life reveals what it means to be human—we are created to be God-dependent people, not self-sufficient people.

Our feelings of inadequacy remind us that we are not God; but celebrating our smallness frees us to depend on God's power.

3. Our Means for Witness—the Holy Spirit

We depend on God's power by "remaining" in Christ (John 15)—he dwells within us through the Holy Spirit.

The "Three Rs":

- ~ *Remember* in every situation that Jesus is with us.

- ~ *Rejoice* that we have access to God's power through Christ (Matthew 28 v 20).
- ~ *Request* the Lord's help in every situation.

God has always used the weak to accomplish his purposes—he can use you too.

TALK NOTES

DISCUSS

1. "God has always used the weak to accomplish his purposes." How have you witnessed this, in your own experience or in those you know? When do you find it hardest to believe the truth of this, and why?

2. How do you respond to the idea that inadequacy is not an obstacle to evangelism—it's a necessity?

3. Remember... Rejoice... Request. How could you start, or keep, consciously practicing the presence of Christ this week? What do you think might change if you do that?

4. What is the one big truth from this session that you will apply to your attitude to evangelism?

NEXT STEPS

- Between now and the next session, consciously practice the presence of Christ, abiding in him by remembering, rejoicing and requesting.
- If you're able to, arrange to meet another member of your group this week to pray together (from now on, we'll call this person your "prayer partner").
- Either with your prayer partner, and/or each day on your own, ask God to grant you both a deeper faith and greater awareness of his power and presence.

PRAY

2

THE CROSS: THE MESS AND THE MIRACLE

INTRO

BIBLE STUDY

Read Luke 23 v 32-49

1. From verses 33-49, Jesus is hanging on a cross—the one who had claimed to be a king is being killed as a criminal. What responses to him does Luke show us?

2. Which of those responses to Jesus' death do you see around you today?

3. What do Jesus' words (each of which would have been agony to utter) show us about his character?

4. *Read 1 Peter 3 v 18.* How could Jesus offer the most lawbreaking man in this scene—a condemned criminal dying at his side—a place "with me in paradise" (Luke 23 v 42)?

5. How does the cross turn upside down the assumptions this world makes about who is powerful... who is good... who needs help... who has eternal life?

TALK

Jesus makes a real difference. But we can't benefit from the cure that Christ brings unless we face the problem—sin (Jeremiah 17 v 9).

Secular culture—and often even our church culture—denies that sin is the problem.

Jesus Died and We Crucified Him (Acts 2 v 23)

All of us are responsible for the death of the only innocent One—so our capacity for sin shouldn't surprise us.

The cross shows us that whatever we have done can be forgiven—because God is willing to forgive us even for the death of Christ.

Jesus Died and We were Crucified with Him (Galatians 2 v 19-20)

On the cross Jesus bore our sin, and our old self was nailed to the cross with him.

We have a new identity—sin no longer defines us.

Walking in the Light of the Cross

We identify and confess our sin.

We are free to love the unlovely, because we suffer from the same disease and need the same cure.

All is grace: remember that no one is beyond the reach of our wonderful Savior.

TALK NOTES

DISCUSS

1. Would a newcomer to your church get the impression that everyone there was a sinner in need of forgiveness, or a good person whose life was sorted? What can you do, as a group or individuals, to make clear that as Christians, you admit the problem as well as offering the answer?

2. How does the "god-complex" display itself in your life?

3. Is there someone you struggle to love, or think is beyond the reach of Christ's forgiveness? How has reflecting on the cross in this situation changed or challenged your attitude?

4. "Jesus died and we crucified him. Never underestimate sin when it cost Jesus his life. But Jesus died and we were crucified with him. Don't overestimate sin either. You're freer than you know."
   What difference will it make to you neither to under- nor overestimate your sin this week?

NEXT STEPS

- Practice explaining why Jesus died on the cross. Aim not to use any words or phrases that someone who has never been to church wouldn't have heard before. And aim to explain it in a single minute.
  If you can, practice with another member of your group, or a friend from church. Even better... ask a non-Christian friend, family member or co-worker if they would mind you practicing with them! You may feel inadequate, but that's OK!

- As you pray over the next few days, ask God to show you three or four non-Christians with whom he would like you to share the gospel. Once you have identified those people, commit to praying for them each day.

PRAY

3

FACING OUR FEARS

INTRO

BIBLE STUDY

God calls Joshua to do something very challenging that will lead to testing, conflict, struggles and pressure. But first God calls and commissions Joshua.

1. How would it help Joshua in his future challenges to know that God had clearly revealed to him his will and pleasure (v 1-4)?

2. After revealing his will, what qualities does God say Joshua needs in order to obey God's purposes (v 5-9)?

How do we obtain these qualities?

Clearly, moral strength and courage are increased by knowing God's will and word, and by trusting God's promises.

3. *Read Matthew 28 v 18-20*. What similar commands and promise does Jesus make to his people here, compared to God's words to Joshua?

4. God knew Joshua would experience fear as he sought to obey God's commands. That is also true for us. We need to be obedient to God and yet realistic about life's challenges. What fears might take hold of us when we share our faith?

What have we learned about what to do when we are afraid?

TALK

The drive to evangelism is a fire within. So...

What Diminishes our Fire?

1. Complacency

Perhaps all our friends are Christians, or we're busy.

2. Confusion

~ Over how to tell the gospel (with our lips and lives)

~ Over who's meant to tell the gospel (Matthew 28 v 19 implies that it is all of us!)

~ Over God's role and our role. God opens eyes and hearts (2 Corinthians 4 v 6; Acts 16 v 14). We are to speak the message and invite people to respond.

3. Fears

Write down your three biggest fears when it comes to evangelism:

1.

2.

3.

The Fear of Offending

~ Be authentic—tell your friend you're worried about offending.

~ Develop a style consistent with your personality.

The Fear of Being Rejected

- Fear is normal, but we must obey despite our fear (Acts 18 v 9)

The Fear of Not Knowing Answers to Questions

- Affirm the question, ask about background and admit your ignorance if necessary!

The Fear of Inconsistencies

- We're not perfect—but we don't need to be.

Our Hidden Fear: What if God doesn't come through?

- Our fears all focus on ourselves; our biggest need is the Spirit's power—God-confidence, not self-confidence.

- Our problem is the sin of unbelief—we must trust that God goes before us.

TALK NOTES

DISCUSS

1. Having heard Becky's talk and thought about your fears, what would you now say are the three fears or factors most likely to stop you talking about Jesus with someone?

2. What have you learned that will help you when you feel afraid?

NEXT STEPS

- Commit to praying frequently, daily, for the people you think Christ is calling you to share his gospel with.

- Continue to pray that God will make you a winsome witness. (Look at the "Praying Powerfully" section on pages 69-70 for help in how to pray).

- Invite one of the people you are praying for to do something this week—it could be as simple as getting a cup of coffee. If the topic of faith naturally arises (and pray it will!), then great. But take this time to build the friendship and to get to know each other better. Aim to gently ask questions about their family background and discover what their interests are.

- As your friendship deepens, try to discover what questions they have about God. What seem to be their resistant points to Christianity?

Note: It may be that, for one reason or another, you need to move through these "Next Steps" more slowly than getting each done between each session. That's fine (as long as it's not just an excuse!). If you need to, move through each set of "Next Steps" at your own pace, so that you'll finish them some time after the course itself finishes.

PRAY

Use these suggestions to pray together as you finish the session, and to include in your prayers on your own this coming week.

- Confess your fears and areas of unbelief that block you from trusting God's power; ask the Lord to enable you to trust that he desires to use you just as you are.

- Ask God to reveal the people in your life who are spiritually open; and to help you to develop genuine friendships and start having easy, lively spiritual discussion.

- Ask God for greater faith in his power and greater dependence on his Spirit; and ask him to make you an effective witness.

4

IT'S ALL ABOUT RELATIONSHIPS

INTRO

BIBLE STUDY

Read Luke 19 v 1-10

Tax collectors worked for the occupying Roman authorities, and they became rich by over-charging their countrymen and keeping the difference for themselves. Unsurprisingly, Jews hated them.

1. So what is surprising about Jesus' treatment of this wealthy tax collector?

2. Why is the crowd's horrified reaction in verse 7 entirely understandable?

3. How does Jesus explain why he has treated Zacchaeus as he has (v 9-10)?

4. What difference does Jesus make to Zacchaeus (v 5-6, 8)?

5. Imagine that "the people" in verse 7 were actually taking this course with you. What might be their attitude towards reaching out to others?

What would Zacchaeus say if he were taking this course a few weeks after meeting Jesus?

TALK

Building authentic relationships with unbelievers is key to evangelism.

The story of the Good Samaritan gives us some profound principles for evangelism (Luke 10 v 25-37).

1. The Kingdom of God is Relational

Jesus sums up life in terms of love relationships—with God and our neighbor.

God didn't hand out flyers to the world—he sent his Son.

God is triune—a relational being.

2. Jesus Radically Identified with People

Jesus had a "go to them"—not "come to us"—approach.

Jesus understood our human experience from the inside out—we must seek to understand our friends' doubts, questions and pain.

Jesus demonstrated that everybody is somebody to God.

Are you involved in authentic friendships where you share your life with unbelieving friends?

3. Jesus was Radically Different—we should be too. How?

We display God's love with our actions.

We depend on God's power through prayer.

We declare God's truth by presenting people with the real Jesus of the Bible—he's irresistible!

TALK NOTES

DISCUSS

1. Do you think that, by character, you tend more towards being radically identified with the world, or radically different? How does Jesus' example help you to be both?

2. "Jesus never treated people as merely evangelistic projects. He established real relationships with real people."
   What stops us establishing real relationships with non-Christians?

3. Imagine someone spent a month living in your house and going with you to your church (on Sundays and any other church activities). From looking at you and your church, what would they conclude matters most to Jesus?

4. Why is it liberating to realize that Jesus calls us to have real friendships with people, rather than to stand aloof, or run in, hit someone with the gospel, and run off again? Are there any changes you need to make in your schedule in order to pursue real, natural relationships with these people?

NEXT STEPS

- Identify (or discuss with your prayer partner) the chief interests of the people you are praying for: music, art, sports, films, food? Again, as the relationship develops, try to understand where they are spiritually. Are they spiritually open, closed, interested, hostile or bored? And why? What do they not understand about Christianity?

- Then plan a casual social activity that you, your prayer partner and at least two seekers could do in the next two weeks. It doesn't matter that they don't know each other. Just invite them to do something they'd like—and then perhaps suggest a meal afterwards. Use the time to get to know each other and have fun! Pray that the topic of faith might come up—but don't push it. One question your friends will probably ask is how you and your Christian friend know each other—and you can casually say, "Oh, we go to the same church" (or something similar).

PRAY

- Ask God to help you understand the needs and questions in the lives of your friends, and to give you a deeper experience and conviction of his love for them.

- Ask God to create in your friends a curiosity about Jesus and a hunger for meaning and purpose.

- Pray that your friends will see something in your life that draws them to God.

5

CULTIVATING CURIOSITY

INTRO

BIBLE STUDY

Read John 4 v 5-30

To understand how Jesus sparked this woman's curiosity, it is important to know that in Jesus' day Jews and Samaritans hated each other. Furthermore, men and women never spoke to each other in public. And religious leaders would be risking their reputation if they spoke publicly to a woman—especially one who (as we learn in verse 18) had been married five times and was now living with a man who wasn't her husband.

1. What does Jesus do that astonishes this Samaritan woman and gets her attention (v 7-9)?

What does it tell us about Jesus that he initiates a conversation with this woman when he is tired, thirsty and hungry?

2. What does Jesus say in verses 10 and 13-14 that cultivates her curiosity? Do you think the woman understands what Jesus is offering (v 15)?

Then, just when the woman asks for this living water, Jesus suddenly delves into her personal life and asks her to go call her husband.

3. Why do you think Jesus wants her to see that her sin is the reason that she needs what he is offering?

If Jesus had given her the "living water" when she first asked for it, she wouldn't have understood what it was and why she needed it. He didn't manipulate her into a premature decision.
When the disciples saw Jesus talking with this woman, they were astonished. They couldn't see what he saw: this woman wasn't a lost cause to God. She had been trying to meet her needs in all the wrong places. Her lifestyle revealed that she was thirsty for God!

4. What lessons and encouragements can we learn for our evangelism from this story?

TALK

1. There is a Process Involved in Evangelism

We cultivate curiosity.

We share the message.

We invite a response.

2. How do we Cultivate Curiosity in the Gospel?

We Cultivate Curiosity by Depending on God's Power (1 Corinthians 4 v 20).

- Pray for yourself—for God's power and authority.
- Pray for your friend—in specific, intelligent ways.
- Pray with your friend—if they share a problem, ask whether they would mind you praying for them right then.

We Cultivate Curiosity through Sharing Truth

- Investigate: ask gentle questions to understand their barriers to faith.
- Stimulate their interest (like Jesus with the Samaritan woman in John 4) by addressing their barriers to faith.

We Cultivate Curiosity through Showing God's Love

3. Raise the Topic of Faith by Asking Good Questions

General interest questions

Specific interest questions (What? Why? How?)

Issue questions—that cause them to reflect on what they believe

"God" questions

TALK NOTES

EXERCISE

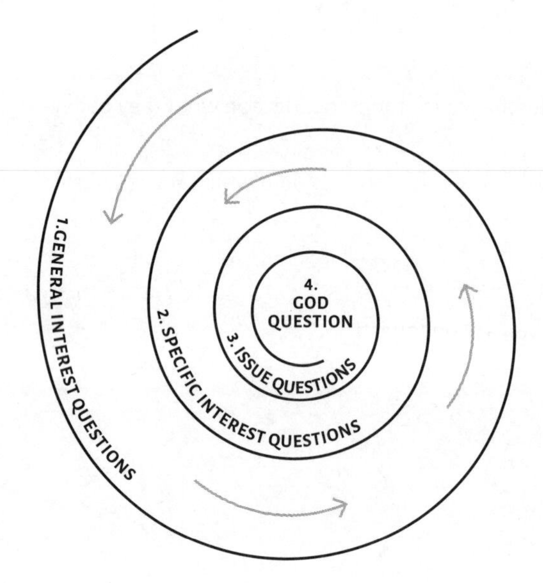

Name:

Interest:

Questions:

1.

2.

3.

4.

NEXT STEPS

- Work out some areas of interest about which you could chat with a friend (or friends), and work out some questions you could ask that will help you move from general to "issue" or "God" questions. Then go ask them the questions!
  Aim to have at least one conversation this week in which you move to asking an "Issue" or even a "God" question. It may seem stilted or awkward at first, but over time you'll get more adept at connecting people's interests and passions with larger issues and even with their consideration of God. Remember, practice makes perfect (or at least proficient!).

- This week, seek to ask at least one of the people you are praying for the "Big Questions" (you'll find the questions on pages 71-72.) You could say, "I heard a speaker at a course we're doing at church say that Christians need to do a better job of listening to and understanding what their friends believe. She gave us some thought-provoking questions to ask our friends. Would you be willing to get a cup of coffee and tell me what you think? I'd be really interested to find out!"
  If they say "Yes" (and most do), then meet twice, over the next couple of weeks, to cover the questions. It's fine to have the questions written on a piece of paper—but don't take notes on their answers! Listen actively, and if you need them to explain further, then say so. Don't offer your opinion unless they ask. This might seem intimidating at first—but people almost universally say they loved the experience. Remember to conclude by saying how much you've enjoyed listening to what they think. Ask if you could meet one more time next week to ask their opinion of some other questions!

PRAY

- Ask God to use you to prompt curiosity about Christian faith in your friends.

- Ask God to guide you to the right person (or people) of whom to ask the "Big Questions," and for courage to speak to them about it; and that these conversations will lead to fruitful, positive discussion about the gospel.

- Pray that you (and your prayer partner if you have one) would be able to gather for a social time together with some friends with whom you feel the Lord is leading you to share more of your life and the gospel.

6

THE GOSPEL: CONTENT AND RESPONSE

INTRO

BIBLE STUDY

Read Acts 2 v 22-41

1. What does Peter say in verses 22-24 about:

   ~ Jesus' life

~ Jesus' death?

~ Jesus' resurrection?

2. How does he challenge the people (v 23, 36)?

How do they react to the news that this Jesus is "both Lord and Messiah"—both God, and the promised King (v 36-37)?

3. What does Peter call them to do in response to the news that Jesus is the risen Lord and Messiah (v 38-40)?

4. What are the three essential points of the gospel that we see in verses 22-24?

5. Peter was talking to Jews who had been in Jerusalem at the time of Jesus' death. The people we talk to are in a very different situation! How would you say the same truths as Peter, and make the same call as Peter, in a way that would connect with those who live and work around you?

TALK ONE

Loving people is important but it's not enough—we need to speak truth.

The gospel can transform lives because it's authored by Christ himself (Galatians 1 v 11-12). It's profound but can be communicated simply.

One outline of the gospel:

1. Creator: The way life was meant to be

God created us to live in intimacy, love and harmony with him and everyone else.

2. Crisis: The mess we made of things

Life on this planet is full of brokenness and suffering.

The first humans rebelled and chose self-rule—and we've done the same.

God's fair but painful judgment is that we suffer the consequences of our sin—in this life and the next.

3. Christ: The cure

On the cross, Jesus took the judgment we deserve.

He was raised to life to offer us a new, dynamic relationship with God.

4. Commitment: God's offer and our response

God offers to forgive all our sins and give us the Holy Spirit.

We must respond to the offer.

5. Completion: The future

One day Jesus will return and make all things new. His people will enjoy God's perfect presence forever.

TALK NOTES

DISCUSS

1. There are many ways to explain the truth of the gospel, including the way Peter did it in Acts 2, and the way Becky communicated it in her talk. There are a few other ideas on pages 73-75 of this book.
   Look through them now in pairs. Then take it in turns to explain the gospel to each other clearly and warmly in a single minute. Tell each other what you each did well, and what you could work on.

2. Dick said in his introduction that one of the tools we need is our testimony—how God worked in us to bring us to faith. Using these "headings," briefly explain to each other your story of faith:

   What life was like before you knew Christ

   The circumstances and/or people God used to start to open your eyes

   How you came into a relationship with Christ

   How Christ has affected your life since then

TALK TWO

God's intention is to transform us. Jesus offers abundant life (John 10 v 10) but warns us to count the cost of following him (Luke 14 v 25-35).

Transformation comes from conversion. Conversion is a mystery!

Our Role...

Watch for the movement of the Spirit.

Speak. Ask, "Is there any reason why you couldn't become a Christian right now?"

Listen to their answer and address any issues they raise.

What is Involved in Making a Commitment to Christ?

The human side: Believing... Repenting... Receiving...

The divine side: Forgiveness of sins and the gift of the Holy Spirit

So someone needs to say:

~ I believe.

~ I am sorry.

~ Come into my life, Jesus.

TALK NOTES

NEXT STEPS

- If you feel that you need more practice, then share the gospel and your conversion story with your prayer partner. Give each other feedback on where you are strong and what you need to work on.

- Aim to get together to ask your friend the second set of "Big Questions" (see pages 71-72).

- Ask God to give you an opportunity to share the gospel message with someone this week (it may be with the person to whom you've been asking the questions, or someone totally unexpected!). Pray that you'll explain it in a way that is faithful, clear and compelling.

PRAY

- Ask God to give you a real understanding and love for the gospel—and the confidence and skill to communicate it clearly.

- Spend time now praising God for the amazing good news of his Son, the Lord Jesus Christ.

- If you asked a friend the "Big Questions" between the last session and this one, pray that your friend will want to continue by answering the second group of questions, and that you will have the opportunity to share the gospel. If you didn't manage to invite a friend to talk through the first set of questions, pray for an opportunity and courage to do so.

7

INTRODUCING THE IRRESISTIBLE JESUS

INTRO

TALK

Jesus is beautiful, radical and controversial! Introduce unbelieving friends to him through a Seeker Bible Study (SBS).

What is a Seeker Bible Study?

A Bible study for anyone with little or no understanding about Christianity, looking at Jesus, where people discover the answers directly from the Bible text.

Why is a Seeker Bible Study Effective?

Most people don't have a clue who Jesus is.

No one has to believe anything in order to come. They can investigate for themselves.

A S.A.F.E. P.L.A.C.E.

~ **S**afe—everyone is accepted

~ **A**uthenticity—they can be who they really are

~ **F**ood and **F**un!

~ **E**veryday language—don't use "God-talk"

~ **P**rocess not pressure; **P**rayer (but not at the start of the study)

~ **L**ove of Christ and **L** ow-key

~ **A**mazed by the relevance of the Bible

~ **C**are for them pastorally—meet up one-to-one

~ **E**veryone is welcome

What are the Advantages for Believers?

You are not posing as the authority, and you don't have to be gifted in evangelism.

Your faith will grow.

Any positive response is positive!

Before leading a study, think through who, what size, where and when.

Inviting people:

- ~ Pray!
- ~ "Have you ever, as an adult, read one of the biographies of Jesus?"
- ~ Suggest getting together just once to start with.
- ~ Make clear they don't need to believe the Bible is historically reliable.

The first meeting:

- ~ Chat and have nibbles and drinks to start
- ~ You could use an SBS guide
- ~ Review the purpose of the group
- ~ At the end, invite people to continue.

TALK NOTES

HOW NOT TO LEAD A SEEKER BIBLE STUDY

Write down everything the co-leaders, Becky and Tim, do *wrong*:

BIBLE STUDY

LUKE 5 v 17-26

Standing room only

Have you ever heard a friend say something like: *"If only I could get my deepest wish fulfilled, then I would be happy"*?

How true do you think that statement is and why?

Historical context

Jesus was extremely controversial in his day. While the common, despised or marginalized people were drawn to him, the religious authorities were frequently incensed by his claims, his associations and his lifestyle.

There were several types of religious leaders in Jesus' day. In this story we are introduced to two significant groups. The Pharisees were a religious sect of Jews who focused on a strict interpretation of the Law of Moses (the first five books of the Bible). The second group, called the teachers of the law (some of whom were also Pharisees), were professionally trained in teaching and applying the law.

We will meet a paralyzed man and his faithful friends, who were so eager for him to be healed of paralysis that they went to where Jesus was teaching in a Galilean town. To their surprise the house was packed not only with local people, but with religious leaders who had traveled from all over the country to listen to this new rabbi who was gaining so much attention. We never learn the paralyzed man's name nor how he developed this condition. Jesus responds to his need in a surprising way.

9

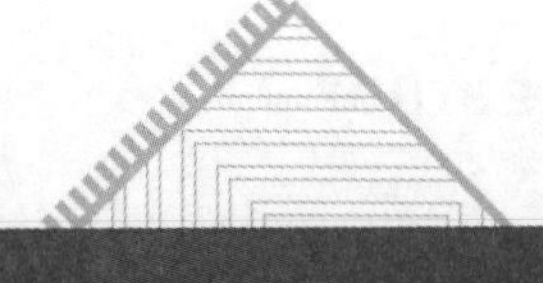

READ SOURCE TEXT: LUKE 5 v 17-26 *THE HEALING OF A PARALYZED MAN*

One day Jesus was teaching, and Pharisees and teachers of the law were sitting there. They had come from every village of Galilee and from Judea and Jerusalem. And the power of the Lord was with Jesus to heal the sick. [18] Some men came carrying a paralyzed man on a mat and tried to take him into the house to lay him before Jesus. [19] When they could not find a way to do this because of the crowd, they went up on the roof and lowered him on his mat through the tiles into the middle of the crowd, right in front of Jesus.

[20] When Jesus saw their faith, he said, "Friend, your sins are forgiven."

[21] The Pharisees and the teachers of the law began thinking to themselves, "Who is this fellow who speaks blasphemy? Who can forgive sins but God alone?"

[22] Jesus knew what they were thinking and asked, "Why are you thinking these things in your hearts? [23] Which is easier: to say, 'Your sins are forgiven,' or to say, 'Get up and walk'? [24] But I want you to know that the Son of Man has authority on earth to forgive sins." So he said to the paralyzed man, "I tell you, get up, take your mat and go home." [25] Immediately he stood up in front of them, took what he had been lying on and went home praising God. [26] Everyone was amazed and gave praise to God. They were filled with awe and said, "We have seen remarkable things today."

Jesus is teaching in the region of the Galilee. The distance from Jerusalem (in the south) to the town of Capernaum (in the north where Jesus was based) is 120 miles. It would take a fit person four or five days to walk that distance!

1. Note where these religious authorities came from (v 17). Why do you think some of the Pharisees and teachers of the law decided to travel such distances and all at the same time?

2. Once the men realize they can't get through the door because of the crowd, what alternative plan do they devise and what are the risks involved (v 18-19)?

❸ What does it say about the paralyzed man and his friends that they were so determined to get to Jesus?

❹ What does Jesus see in these men that impresses him (v 20a)?

❺ When Jesus says the man's sins are forgiven (v 20b), what do you think the reaction of the paralytic and his friends might have been?

❻ Jesus seems to be saying to this man: "If all I do is heal your body, the happiness won't last, because the root of your problem is deeper than your physical condition." What do you think about this?

❼ By saying that his sins were forgiven, what did these religious leaders correctly perceive about the controversial claim Jesus was indirectly making (v 21)?

The religious leaders were amazed by Jesus' healing ministry. But they were outraged by his claim to forgive sin, because they knew that was something only God could do. Jesus didn't say to the paralyzed man: "Look, we all blow it. Nobody's perfect, so just take heart in that." Instead, Jesus proclaimed that the sins of the paralyzed man were forgiven, simply because he had pronounced it so! It was an earth-shattering statement that reflected Jesus' identity and mission—which wasn't lost on the Pharisees!

But what Jesus does next shocks them even more. When the Old Testament religious leaders wanted to invoke authority, they would always cite divine (never personal) authority by saying: "Thus says the Lord." The religious leaders believed the worst sin of all was to commit blasphemy—the claim to be God.

❽ What authority did Jesus invoke when he spoke to the paralytic (v 24b)?

So, why does this matter?

C. S. Lewis, an Oxford professor and Christian writer who was once a fervent atheist, wrote:

> *"Then comes the real shock. Among the Jews there suddenly turns up a man who goes about talking as if he was God. He claims to forgive sins. He says he always existed. He says he is coming to judge the world at the end of time ... and when you have grasped that, you will see that what this man said was, quite simply, the most shocking thing that has ever been uttered by human lips."*

Why do you think people who reject the controversial claims that Jesus made about his own identity still call him a great teacher and leader?

Notes

13

GOODBYE!

REFLECTION: AS YOU FINISH...

1. If you had to sum up in one sentence how this course has changed how you think and feel about evangelism, what would it be?

2. In what ways is the Spirit prompting you to change in some way, in order to share Christ with those around you?

3. What are the biggest dangers that would stop you living out what you've seen in the Bible during these sessions? How will you resist those dangers?

NEXT STEPS

- Pray about whether there is someone (or some people) you could invite to a Seeker Bible Study. Speak to others in the group to see whether you could form a group with one or two others and their non-Christian friends who would like to come.

PRAY

- Thank God for what you have learned during this course.
- Ask God to use you to lead one person to Christ during this year!
- Ask God to guide you about starting a Seeker Bible Study, and whether you should invite another Christian in your group to lead it with you, so that both of you can bring your friends.

EXTRA RESOURCES

PRAYING POWERFULLY

God "is able to do immeasurably more than all we ask or imagine, according to his power that is at work within us" (Ephesians 3 v 20-21). So you need to and can pray confidently what Paul did: "that whenever I speak, words may be given me so that I will fearlessly make known the mystery of the gospel, for which I am an ambassador..." (Ephesians 6 v 19-20). Praying powerfully is about praying to our powerful Father in the ways he has taught us to pray in his word.

Which non-Christians has God placed in your life? What is their central interest in life? (For example, sports, family, the arts, education, technology, retirement, business.)

Friends:

Relatives:

Neighbors:

Colleagues:

Ask God to work in them to:

- ~ create a hunger in them for God.
- ~ open their eyes to the emptiness of life without him.
- ~ help them to be aware of their need.
- ~ open their hearts to be willing to have a spiritual conversation.
- ~ protect them from the enemy's devices.
- ~ bless them in specific ways they need.

Ask God to work in you to:

- ~ help you live a consistent and attractive Christian life.
- ~ make you a person others want to talk to because of your authenticity.
- ~ increase your courage and your faith that he will use you just as you are.

BIG QUESTIONS

Week One: Questions about God and Faith

(Select the questions you feel are most appropriate for the person.)

1. When it comes to spiritual matters, would you describe yourself as unconvinced, interested or a believer, and why?

2. Just for the sake of argument—suppose there is a God. What would you want this God to be like?

3. If there is a God and you could ask him one question, what would it be?

4. Does the idea of having faith in a God we can't see strike you as superstitious? Do you think we might operate by "faith" in some areas of our life without realizing it? Do you ever trust in things you can't see or prove?

5. According to the Bible, we all worship something—whether it's God or success or family etc. Do you think that is true? (If they seem open, you might say, "May I share some things I used to put my trust in before becoming a Christian, and still find it easy to put my trust in today?")

Remember to conclude by telling them how much you've enjoyed listening to what they say. Ask if you could meet one more time next week!

Week Two: Questions on the Human Problem and Jesus Christ

1. What do you think is the biggest problem in the world today? What is the solution? *They will probably say that the problem is either external or internal. If they say the problem is internal (e.g. we are greedy, or selfish) and the solution is external (we need more education) then you might point that out. For example, one Christian using these questions said to their friend, "Hmm, but if, as you say, we are ALL greedy, and the solution is education—then who's going to teach the class?!"*

2. Who do you think Jesus really was? What do you base this on?
   If they ask, "But how do we even know that he really lived?" then feel free to say that there is credible historical evidence that backs up his life and claims and the things he is reported to have done. These historical records of course include the Bible, but also Jewish historians like Josephus and Roman historians such as Tacitus.

3. Have you ever read the biblical accounts of the life of Jesus? What did you think? Did it make any sense?

4. Have you ever had an experience in which you felt God was there or making himself known to you?

5. I'm currently doing a course with some friends at my church, and one thing the course presenters encouraged us to do is to ask a friend if we could take a few minutes to share the essence of the Christian message with them. I don't know that I'll be very good at this, but would you be willing to listen, and then give me feedback on where I was clear and what didn't make sense?

HELPFUL WAYS TO OUTLINE THE GOSPEL

Along with the Creation - Crisis - Christ - Commitment - Completion outline given in Talk One in Session Six, there are countless great ways to explain the gospel to someone. Here are just a few, ranging from very simple to more visual:

CHRIST JESUS

The message of Christianity can be summed up by these two names:

"Christ" means God's promised, all-powerful, eternal King. Christ came to show how great it is to be under his perfect, loving rule—but the fact that there is a Christ is concerning, for none of us have lived under his rule, preferring to rule ourselves. Christ will rule his perfect kingdom forever, but we face being excluded from it because we have rejected him.

But...

"Jesus" means God rescues. Christ did not come only to show his kingdom, but to open his kingdom. He died and rose again so that we can be forgiven and restored to relationship with him, living under his rule. He rescues us from exclusion from his kingdom, and to enjoy his kingdom with him forever.

So to come into his kingdom, all we need to do is recognize him as Christ—our King, who is to be in charge of our lives—and to trust him as Jesus—our God-sent rescuer, who forgives and restores us.

DO / DONE

This outline can be done with a scrap of paper or a napkin:

Write "DO": There's no doubt that there is something wrong with the world—just look around you. Humans are not in good relationship with each other, with the world, or most importantly of all, with God.

All world religions seek to confront that problem, and they can all be summed up in two letters—"DO." They teach what we must "DO" to be restored to relationship with God. But the problem is that we can never know if we are doing the right things, or enough of the right things—and in fact the Bible says that "all have sinned and fall short of the glory of God" (Romans 3 v 23). We can never DO enough.

But the message of Christianity is uniquely different. It is summed up by four letters: "DONE." Christianity teaches that what we could not do, God has done for us, by sending Jesus, his Son. Jesus lived a perfect life, and then he died to take the punishment for all our sin—our rejection of God and his rule. "God demonstrates his own love for us in this: while we were still sinners, Christ died for us" (Romans 5 v 8). So to be restored to eternal relationship with God, we need to stop trying to DO good things to earn it, and simply trust that Jesus has DONE all we need to enjoy it.

THE BARRIER BROKEN

"God saw all that he had made, and it was very good."

Genesis 1 v 31

God made people to enjoy perfect life in his world, in relationship with him, under his loving rule, forever.

GOD

HUMANS

"All have sinned and fall short of the glory of God." *Romans 3 v 23*

We reject God's loving rule—we sin. This means we don't know God and are separated from enjoying perfect life with him, now and in the future.

GOD

J

HUMANS

"The Word was God ... The Word became flesh and made his dwelling among us." *John 1 v 1, 14*

Jesus Christ lived on earth as a man. He is the "Word"—God's Son, who has always lived under his Father's loving rule. He reveals to us what God is like and shows how great life in relationship with God is.

GOD
J
HUMANS

"Christ ... suffered once for sins, the righteous for the unrighteous, to bring you to God." *1 Peter 3 v 18*

Jesus died on a cross. He took the punishment of separation from God that we deserve as sinful ("unrighteous") people, so that he can give us a right relationship with God.

GOD
S
HUMANS

"God has raised this Jesus to life ... he has received from the Father the promised Holy Spirit and has poured [him] out." *Acts 2 v 32-33*

God raised his Son, Jesus, back to life. He returned to heaven and sent his Spirit into the world, to enable people to know him and live under his loving rule.

"Serve the living and true God, and ... wait for his Son from heaven ... Jesus, who rescues us from the coming wrath." *1 Thessalonians 1 v 9-10*

Christians are people who:

- *turn* away from rejecting God's loving rule, and try to serve him.
- *wait* for his Son to return, to remake and rule the world so that it's perfect again.
- *know* they will not face God's anger at their sin (his "wrath"), because Jesus has rescued them by being punished in their place on the cross.

Other great gospel explanations can be found online at:

evangelism.intervarsity.org/how/gospel-outline/big-story-tutorial-video

navigators.org/Tools/Evangelism%20Resources/Tools/The%20Bridge%20to%20Life

APOLOGETICS: RESOURCES FOR ANSWERING TOUGH QUESTIONS

General

Books:

The Reason for God (Tim Keller)
If You Could Ask God One Question (Paul Williams and Barry Cooper)
Hope Has Its Reasons (Rebecca Manley Pippert)
What Kind of God? (Michael Ots)
Fool's Talk (Os Guinness)
Can Man Live Without God? (Ravi Zacharias)
The Twilight of Atheism (Alister McGrath)

Something short:

Good Question (Carl Laferton)

Online:

bethinking.org
christianityexplored.org/tough-questions
rzim.org/just-thinking-broadcasts

The Reliability of the Bible

Why Trust the Bible? (Amy Orr-Ewing)
Can We Really Trust the Bible? (Barry Cooper)
Is God a Moral Monster? (Paul Copan)

Science and Faith

God's Undertaker (John Lennox)
Unnatural Enemies (Kirsty Birkett)
Who Made God? (Edgar Andrews)

Sexual Ethics

Is God Anti-Gay? (Sam Allberry)
What is the Meaning of Sex? (Denny Burk)

The Problem of Suffering and Evil

Unspeakable (Os Guinness)
If I Were God, I'd End all the Pain (John Dickson)
Why Suffering? (Ravi Zacharias and Vince Vitale)
Why? (Sharon Dirckx)

The Resurrection

The Case for Christ (Lee Strobel)
Raised? (Jonathan Dodson)

Other Religions

Jesus Among Other Gods (Ravi Zacharias)
Seeking Allah, Finding Jesus (Nabeel Qureshi)
No God But One (Nabeel Quereshi)
If I were God, I'd Make Myself Clearer (John Dickson)

Intolerance

Is the Bible Intolerant? (Amy Orr-Ewing)
The Intolerance of Tolerance (Don Carson)

Relativism and Truth

True for You, but not for Me (Paul Copan)

Worldview

Naming the Elephant (James Sire)
The Universe Next Door (James Sire)
What's Your Worldview? (James Anderson)

Becky Pippert MINISTRIES

Becky's years of experience of talking to people about Jesus shine through on each page of these Bible studies, written for Christians to walk through with their non-Christian friends. These "Seeker Bible Studies" have proven incredibly effective in bringing people around the world to see who Jesus is, and what he is offering to them.

Uncovering the Life of Jesus contains six studies in the Gospel of Luke. *Discovering the Real Jesus* comprises seven encounters with Jesus from John's Gospel.

thegoodbook.com | thegoodbook.co.uk | thegoodbook.com.au

Voted by *Christianity Today* as one of the books that have shaped evangelical Christians in the past 50 years. Becky's insights and stories still speak to our hearts, minds and lives thirty years after this book was first published.

amazon.com | thegoodbook.co.uk

LIVEDIFFERENT

This realistic and humorous book will help prepare and encourage you to be honest and bold in your evangelism, presenting the gospel fully and properly, even when it's tough.

"A great read that is both realistic and hopeful about our evangelism, written by a man whom God has used mightily to spread the gospel. Every Christian will benefit from this."
Becky Pippert

thegoodbook.com | thegoodbook.co.uk

At The Good Book Company, we are dedicated to helping Christians and local churches grow. We believe that God's growth process always starts with hearing clearly what he has said to us through his timeless word—the Bible.

Ever since we opened our doors in 1991, we have been striving to produce resources that honor God in the way the Bible is used. We have grown to become an international provider of user-friendly resources to the Christian community, with believers of all backgrounds and denominations using our Bible studies, books, evangelistic resources, DVD-based courses and training events.

We want to equip ordinary Christians to live for Christ day by day, and churches to grow in their knowledge of God, their love for one another, and the effectiveness of their outreach.

Call us for a discussion of your needs or visit one of our local websites for more information on the resources and services we provide.

Your friends at The Good Book Company

NORTH AMERICA	thegoodbook.com	866 244 2165
UK & EUROPE	thegoodbook.co.uk	0333 123 0880
AUSTRALIA	thegoodbook.com.au	(02) 6100 4211
NEW ZEALAND	thegoodbook.co.nz	(+64) 3 343 2463

WWW.CHRISTIANITYEXPLORED.ORG
Our partner site is a great place for those exploring the Christian faith, with a clear explanation of the good news, powerful testimonies and answers to difficult questions.